Delaware
The First State

Tika Downey

PowerKiDS press™

New York

Published in 2010 by The Rosen Publishing Group, Inc.
29 East 21st Street, New York, NY 10010

First Edition

Editor: Joanne Randolph
Book Design: Greg Tucker
Layout Design: Kate Laczynski
Photo Researcher: Jessica Gerweck

Photo Credits: Cover © Kevin Fleming/Corbis; p. 5 Brian Gordon Green/Getty Images; p. 7 MPI/Getty Images; p. 9 © www.istockphoto.com/Elisa Frank; pp. 11, 22 (bird, flower, tree) Shutterstock.com; pp. 13, 15 Jake Rajs/Getty Images; p. 17 © Robert J. Bennett/age fotostock; p. 19 © SuperStock/age fotostock; p. 22 (fish) Roger Phillips/Getty Images; p. 22 (Caesar Augustus Rodney) p. 22 (Mary Ann Shadd Cary) Jerry Pinkney/National Geographic/Getty Images; p. 22 (Henry Heimlich) Dan Callister/Getty Images.

Library of Congress Cataloging-in-Publication Data

Downey, Tika.
  Delaware : the First State / Tika Downey.
      p. cm. — (Our amazing states)
  Includes index.
  ISBN 978-1-4358-9356-6 (library binding) — ISBN 978-1-4358-9808-0 (pbk.) — ISBN 978-1-4358-9809-7 (6-pack)
  1. Delaware—Juvenile literature. I. Title.
  F164.3.D69 2010
  975.1—dc22
                                          2009033415

Manufactured in the United States of America

CPSIA Compliance Information: Batch #WW10PK: For Further Information contact Rosen Publishing, New York, New York at 1-800-237-9932

Contents

The First State

Delaware is the second-smallest state. Only Rhode Island is smaller. Delaware has fewer people than many other states, too. Only five states have fewer people.

Delaware shares a small **peninsula** on the Atlantic coast with parts of Maryland and Virginia. The peninsula is named Delmarva after the three states. Delaware's name comes from a Virginia sailor who discovered a new bay in 1610. He named it in honor of Virginia's governor Lord De La Warr.

Do you know why Delaware is called the First State? It is because it was the first colony to agree to the U.S. **Constitution**. That made Delaware the young nation's first state. Today, the state's people honor the event every year during Delaware Day.

Delaware's Harbor of Refuge Lighthouse sits on Cape Henlopen and is an active lighthouse. The tower, built in 1926, is 76 feet (23 m) tall.

Delaware's Past

People have lived in Delaware for thousands of years. When Europeans arrived in the 1600s, Lenapes, Susquehannocks, and other Native Americans were living there.

The first European to see Delaware was likely Henry Hudson in 1609. Swedes founded the first lasting European colony in 1638 at modern-day Wilmington. England took control of Delaware in 1664.

In 1775, the colonies began fighting for freedom from England. They won their freedom in 1783 and became the United States. The young nation's leaders wrote the Constitution in 1787. On December 7, Delaware became the first state to agree to it.

William Penn, who founded the colony of Pennsylvania, trades for land with the Delaware Native Americans in 1682. He used the land to found Dover.

Land and Weather

Delaware has cool winters and hot, **humid** summers. It gets almost 4 feet (120 cm) of rain yearly! Only about half the days are sunny.

The low, flat Atlantic Coastal Plain covers most of Delaware. This means most of Delaware's land is low and flat, too. The state's highest point, Ebright Azimuth, is only about 448 feet (137 m) tall. Many buildings are taller than that!

Sandy beaches, **marshes**, and bays line the coast. The largest bays are the Delaware, Rehoboth, and Indian River bays. Delaware has many rivers, too, including the Delaware, Christina, Nanticoke, Indian, and Pocomoke rivers. Southern Delaware has large **swamps**.

Rehoboth Beach is one of Delaware's best-known and most visited beaches. Rehoboth has a boardwalk, hotels, places to eat, and more.

Delaware's Wild Side

Besides its beautiful beaches, Delaware has forests with oak, wild cherry, pine, **bald cypress**, and other trees as well as wildflowers and wild berries. Many animals are at home in Delaware's forests, fields, marshes, and swamps. Some of the animals you might see are deer, otters, foxes, **muskrats**, and snapping turtles. The coastal waters have clams and crabs, including the state **marine** animal, the horseshoe crab.

Can you guess how the horseshoe crab got its name? Its body is shaped like a horse's hoof! These animals are called living **fossils** because they have lived since the time of dinosaurs. They eat marine worms and clams. In turn, they are eaten by shorebirds.

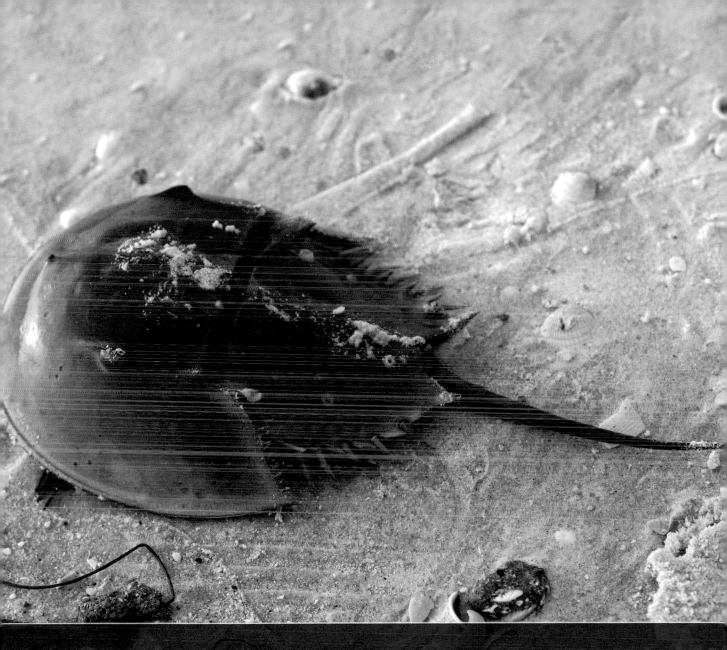

People use matter from horseshoe crabs to check for poisons in drugs and even to make bandages!

Beautiful Bombay Hook

On the coast of Delaware Bay is one of Delaware's most interesting wild places, Bombay Hook National Wildlife **Refuge**. The refuge is mostly tidal salt marsh, although it also has ponds, forests, swamps, and fields. It was set aside to give **migrating** birds a safe place to rest and raise their young. You can see almost 280 kinds of birds there, including waterbirds and songbirds.

Birds are not the only animals that make their homes in the refuge. You might see bats, foxes, woodchucks, beavers, and muskrats. If you are very lucky, you might even see flying squirrels or seals in the bay! The refuge has salamanders, frogs, turtles, and snakes, too.

Hundreds of snow geese, shown here, come to the Bombay Hook refuge during their winter migration. In the summer, snow geese live in the Arctic.

Delaware Businesses

Wilmington, Delaware's largest city, is the state's banking center. Banking is one of Delaware's biggest businesses. There are also factories in Delaware. If you have taken drugs when you were sick, they might have come from Delaware. You might have eaten sweet foods made in Delaware, too. Other companies make cars, cloth, paper, rubber goods, plastic goods, and metal goods.

Delaware farms are famous for their chickens. They also produce other kinds of food, such as corn, milk, peas, and spinach. Delaware fishermen catch many kinds of fish, as well as clams, crabs, eels, and snails!

Delaware has more than 2,000 farms with an average farm size of around 230 acres (93 ha).
The two main crops grown are soybeans and corn.

A Look at Dover

Do you know who William Penn was? He founded Pennsylvania. He also founded Dover, Delaware, in 1683. The city was laid out in 1717 and became Delaware's capital in 1777.

Dover is known for its old, historic buildings that remind visitors of the state's past. The Old State House, built in 1792, held the early government offices. In 1933, the government moved into **Legislative** Hall, which faces the Old State House. Besides government offices, the hall holds paintings of scenes from Delaware's history. Dover also has a church from 1790 and the 1740 house that was colonial leader John Dickinson's boyhood home.

Although it was built in the early 1930s, Legislative Hall was built to match the city's old buildings. It is made with handmade bricks.

The Hagley Museum and Library

In Wilmington, Delaware, you can visit the Hagley Museum and Library and learn about the history of American business. The museum was once the site of the gunpowder works founded by E. I. du Pont de Nemours. Du Pont was a chemist and gunpowder maker in France, who moved to America in 1800.

Set on the shores of the Brandywine River, the Hagley Museum brings early American **industry** to life through its mill, machine shop, and a workers' community. Visitors can also see the home and gardens of the du Pont family. Du Pont's company is now one of the leading chemical companies in the country.

The Hagley Museum and Library sits on 235 acres (95 ha) of land. They offer hands-on activities and a firsthand look at the birth of American industry.

Delaware Is Delightful

   Tiny Delaware has much to offer visitors. On the coast, people can play on beaches, swim, or watch migrating birds. Visitors can also enjoy outdoor activities at Great Cypress Swamp and other state parks and wildlife areas.

   Delaware is a great place to learn about our nation's history. The graveyard of New Castle's Immanuel Church has many colonial leaders' graves. In Wilmington, you can see a copy of a famous old ship that brought Swedish settlers to Delaware. Delaware has art museums, too, such as the Biggs Museum of American Art, in Dover. What would you like to do in Delaware?

Glossary

bald cypress (BAWLD SY-pres) A kind of large tree that grows in swamps and has flat, pointed needles instead of leaves.

Constitution (kon-stih-TOO-shun) The basic rules by which the United States is governed.

fossils (FAH-sulz) The hardened remains of dead animals or plants.

humid (HYOO-med) Wet or moist.

industry (IN-dus-tree) A business in which many people work and make money producing something.

legislative (LEH-jis-lay-tiv) Having to do with the branch of government that makes laws and collects taxes.

marine (muh-REEN) Having to do with the sea.

marshes (MAHRSH-ez) Areas of soft, wet land.

migrating (MY-gray-ting) Moving from place to place as the seasons change.

muskrats (MUSK-rats) Rats that live in the water.

peninsula (peh-NIN-suh-luh) An area of land surrounded by water on three sides.

refuge (REH-fyooj) A place that gives shelter or security.

swamps (SWOMPS) Wet lands with a lot of trees and bushes.

Delaware State Symbols

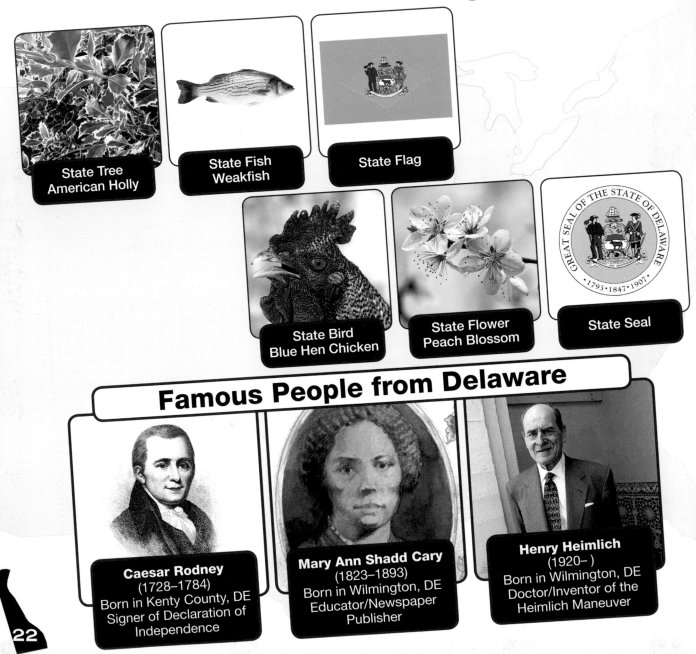

State Tree
American Holly

State Fish
Weakfish

State Flag

State Bird
Blue Hen Chicken

State Flower
Peach Blossom

State Seal

GREAT SEAL OF THE STATE OF DELAWARE
·1793·1847·1907·

Famous People from Delaware

Caesar Rodney
(1728–1784)
Born in Kenty County, DE
Signer of Declaration of
Independence

Mary Ann Shadd Cary
(1823–1893)
Born in Wilmington, DE
Educator/Newspaper
Publisher

Henry Heimlich
(1920–)
Born in Wilmington, DE
Doctor/Inventor of the
Heimlich Maneuver

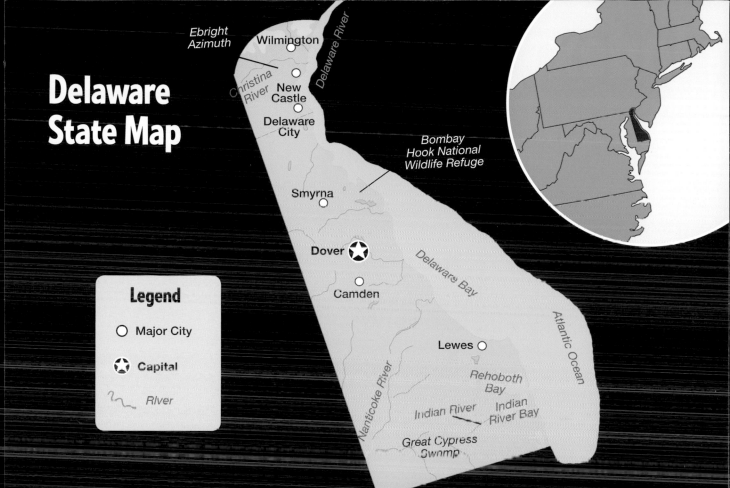

Delaware State Map

Ebright
Azimuth

Wilmington

Delaware River

Christina
River

New
Castle

Delaware
City

Bombay
Hook National
Wildlife Refuge

Smyrna

Dover ★

Delaware Bay

Camden

Atlantic Ocean

Lewes ○

Nanticoke River

Rehoboth
Bay

Indian River

Indian
River Bay

Great Cypress
Swamp

Legend

○ Major City

★ Capital

〰 River

Delaware State Facts

Nickname: The First State

Population: 873,092

Area: 2,057 square miles (5,328 sq km)

Motto: "Liberty and Independence"

Song: "Our Delaware," words by George B. Hynson and music
by Will M. S. Brown

Index

Web Sites

Due to the changing nature of Internet links, PowerKids Press has developed an online list of Web sites related to the subject of this book. This site is updated regularly. Please use this link to access the list:

www.powerkidslinks.com/amst/de/

24